Student Success Toolbox

Improving Learning and Performance through Assessment

First Edition

published by

Pacific Crest
Hampton, NH

Student Success Toolbox

Improving Learning and Performance through Assessment

First Edition

Layout, Production, and Cover Design by Denna Hintze

Copyright © 2013

Pacific Crest
P.O. Box 370
Hampton, NH 03843
603-601-2246
www.pcrest.com

No part of this publication may be reproduced, stored in a retrieval system, or transmitted in any form or by any means (electronic, mechanical, photocopying, recording, or otherwise) without the prior written permission of the author and copyright holder.

ISBN: 978-1-60263-112-0

Table of Contents

General Tools 1
- Log of Entries 3
- Glossary 5
- Concept Map Form 11
  - *sample* 12
- Addressing & Avoiding Errors 13
  - *sample* 16
- Reading Log (2) 17
  - *sample* 21
- Learning Journal (3) 23
  - *sample* 26
- Mentoring Planning 27
- Mentoring Agreement 28

Team Tools 29
- Introduction to Forming Teams and Team Roles 30
- Reflector Report (3) 33
  - *sample* 36
- Recorder Report (2) 37
  - *sample* 41
- Weekly Reflector Report 43
- Weekly Recorder Report 45

Performance Improvement Tools 47
- Continuum of Performance Levels 48
- SII Self-Assessment Report (3) 49
  - *sample* 52
- SII Performance Assessment Report (2) 53
  - *sample* 57
- SII Team Assessment Report (3) 59
  - *sample* 62
- Getting a Handle on Performance: The Performance Model 63
- Performance Analysis and Assessment (2) 64
  - *sample* 66
- Preparation Worksheet 67
  - *sample* 69

Course Tools 71
- How to be an "A" Student 72
- Course Record Sheet 73
- Weekly Planner (2) 75
- Blank Calendar (3) 77
  - *Beginning:* Analyzing a Course Syllabus (Activity) 80
  - Learning Contract 83
  - *Mid-Term:* Mid-Term Assessment Form 85
  - *Closure:* Course Assessment 87
- Classification of Learning Skills 89

Improving Learning and Performance through Assessment

*While this book will work well on
its own, the companion web site:*

www.studentsuccesstoolbox.com

*provides access to additional tools, blank
forms, rubrics, methodologies, and more!*

General Tools

Log of Entries

Glossary

Concept Map Form

Addressing & Avoiding Errors

Reading Log

Learning Journal

Mentoring Planning

Mentoring Agreement

Improving Learning and Performance through Assessment

Feel free to use this page for notes!

Name _____

Course _____

Semester/Term _____

Log of Entries

Date	Page	Activity	Summary of Entry

Copyright © 2013 Pacific Crest

Date	Page	Activity	Summary of Entry

Transfer new vocabulary words, specialized phrases, formulas, and important calculations to this section.

Glossary

Word or Term **Definition, proper use, explanation, source, and page**

A-B

C-D

Word or Term **Definition, proper use, explanation, source, and page**

E-G

Improving Learning and Performance through Assessment

H-K

Word or Term   **Definition, proper use, explanation, source, and page**

L-M

N-P

Word or Term   **Definition, proper use, explanation, source, and page**

Q-S

Improving Learning and Performance through Assessment

T-V

Word or Term   **Definition, proper use, explanation, source, and page**

W-Z

Numerical

Formula or Key Idea	Definition, proper use, explanation, source, and page

Concept Map Form

Name or Team Members:

Concept

Associated Concepts

Improving Learning and Performance through Assessment

Sample Concept Map of "Concept Maps"

Concept maps are graphical tools for organizing and representing knowledge. They include concepts, usually enclosed in circles or boxes of some type, and relationships between concepts indicated by a connecting line linking two concepts. Words on the line, referred to as linking words or linking phrases, specify the relationship between the two concepts. (From: Novak, J. D. & A. J. Cañas, The Theory Underlying Concept Maps and How to Construct Them, Technical Report IHMC CmapTools 2006-01 Rev 01-2008, Florida Institute for Human and Machine Cognition, 2008" available at: http://cmap.ihmc.us/Publications/ResearchPapers/TheoryUnderlyingConceptMaps.pdf.)

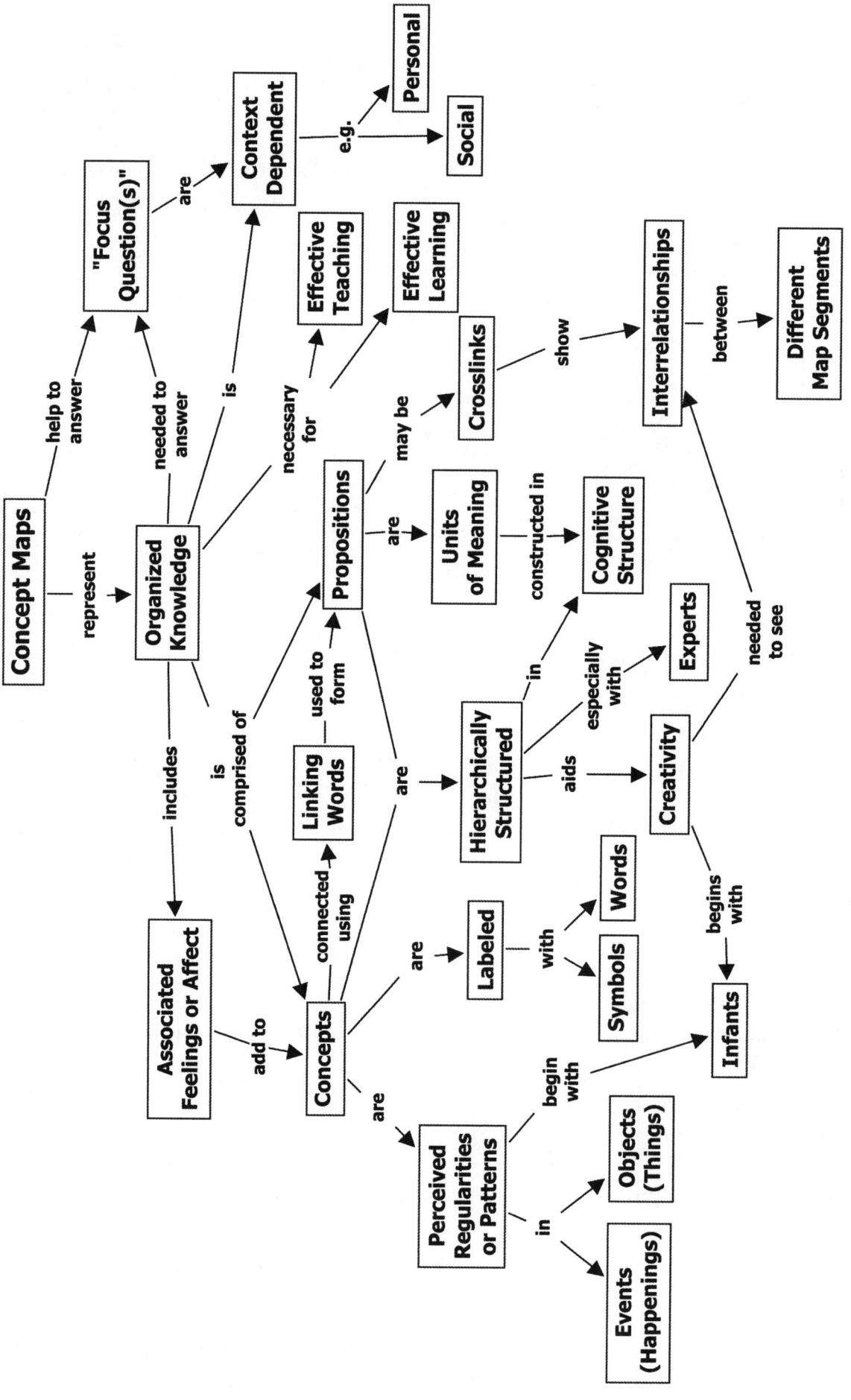

Student Success Toolbox

Name _____

Focus or Course _____

OOPS! Addressing & Avoiding Errors

Error description examples: Misapplication of a Rule, Incorrect Assumption, Failure to Follow Instructions, Lack of Understanding, etc.

Error Description (What kind of error is this?)	**Example of Error** (demonstrate the error; use a diagram/drawing if needed)	**Context where error occurs** (When do you make this error?)
Reason for error (Why do you make this error?)	**Correct Procedure** (correction of example shown above)	**How I will avoid making this error in the future**

Error Description (What kind of error is this?)	**Example of Error** (demonstrate the error; use a diagram/drawing if needed)	**Context where error occurs** (When do you make this error?)
Reason for error (Why do you make this error?)	**Correct Procedure** (correction of example shown above)	**How I will avoid making this error in the future**

Copyright © 2013 Pacific Crest

Name _____

Focus or Course _____

Addressing & Avoiding Errors

OOPS!

Error description examples: Misapplication of a Rule, Incorrect Assumption, Failure to Follow Instructions, Lack of Understanding, etc.

Error Description (What kind of error is this?)	**Example of Error** (demonstrate the error; use a diagram/drawing if needed)	**Context where error occurs** (When do you make this error?)
Reason for error (Why do you make this error?)	**Correct Procedure** (correction of example shown above)	**How I will avoid making this error in the future**

Error Description (What kind of error is this?)	**Example of Error** (demonstrate the error; use a diagram/drawing if needed)	**Context where error occurs** (When do you make this error?)
Reason for error (Why do you make this error?)	**Correct Procedure** (correction of example shown above)	**How I will avoid making this error in the future**

Copyright © 2013 Pacific Crest

Name _____

Focus or Course _____

OOPS! Addressing & Avoiding Errors

Error description examples: Misapplication of a Rule, Incorrect Assumption, Failure to Follow Instructions, Lack of Understanding, etc.

Error Description (What kind of error is this?)	**Example of Error** (demonstrate the error; use a diagram/drawing if needed)	**Context where error occurs** (When do you make this error?)
Reason for error (Why do you make this error?)	**Correct Procedure** (correction of example shown above)	**How I will avoid making this error in the future**

Error Description (What kind of error is this?)	**Example of Error** (demonstrate the error; use a diagram/drawing if needed)	**Context where error occurs** (When do you make this error?)
Reason for error (Why do you make this error?)	**Correct Procedure** (correction of example shown above)	**How I will avoid making this error in the future**

Copyright © 2013 Pacific Crest

Name _____

Focus or Course _____

Addressing & Avoiding Errors

samples OOPS!

Error description examples: Misapplication of a Rule, Incorrect Assumption, Failure to Follow Instructions, Lack of Understanding, etc.

Error Description (What kind of error is this?)	**Example of Error** (demonstrate the error; use a diagram/drawing if needed)	**Context where error occurs** (When do you make this error?)
Using an apostrophe for the possessive of "it" Misapplication of a Rule	The cat ate (it's) food.	I make this error each time I use the possessive form of "it".

Reason for error (Why do you make this error?)	**Correct Procedure** (correction of example shown above)	**How I will avoid making this error in the future**
I don't distinguish between "it" possessive (belonging to) and the contraction of "it is"	The cat ate its food.	ANY time I write "its" I will think, "Use an apostrophe ONLY if I mean IT IS."

Error Description (What kind of error is this?)	**Example of Error** (demonstrate the error; use a diagram/drawing if needed)	**Context where error occurs** (When do you make this error?)
Not placing the decimal correctly in the answer to a decimal calculation. Calculation Error	The decimal point is in the wrong position in the answer. I should have counted 4 places from the right-most digit. $^1^1$ 0.312 × 1.5 1560 03120 .04680	I tend to make this error when there is a leading or ending zero in ANY of the numbers (factors OR their product).

Reason for error (Why do you make this error?)	**Correct Procedure** (correction of example shown above)	**How I will avoid making this error in the future**
I do not carefully count the decimal places in the factors so that I can place it correctly in their product.	$^1^1$ 0.312 × 1.5 1560 03120 0.4680 4 places	I'll review my work, counting decimal places in problems, writing down that number. Then I'll draw arrows showing the decimal moving, place by place, for EVERY problem until carefully counting places becomes a habit.

Student Success Toolbox

Book/Title, Pages

Reading Log

Name _____

Date _____

1 My **purpose** is: _____

2 My **learning objectives** are:

3 My **performance criteria** are:

4 **Time** I expect to spend reading: _____

5 Key **Vocabulary**   Use each key word in a new context or phrase.

_____   _____
_____   _____
_____   _____
_____   _____

6 **Outline** of reading (structure):

7 **Quick read** (information about the reading and questions I have as I begin to read):

Copyright © 2013 Pacific Crest

continued on other side

17

8 **Comprehensive Read** **Actual Time** I spent reading: _____

9 **Inquiry Questions**   Questions, ideas, opinions, discoveries:

10 **Synthesis**   Pull it together:

11 **Integrate**   The relationship between the new information and my previous knowledge and experience is:

12 **Assessment**   The following affected (positively or negatively) the quality of my reading performance and how I can improve:

INSTRUCTOR FEEDBACK

Strengths:

Areas for Improvement:

Insights:

Student Success Toolbox

Book/Title, Pages

Reading Log

Name _____

Date _____

1 My **purpose** is: _____

2 My **learning objectives** are:

3 My **performance criteria** are:

4 **Time** I expect to spend reading: _____

5 Key **Vocabulary**   Use each key word in a new context or phrase.

_____   _____
_____   _____
_____   _____
_____   _____

6 **Outline** of reading (structure):

7 **Quick read** (information about the reading and questions I have as I begin to read):

Copyright © 2013 Pacific Crest

continued on other side

19

8 **Comprehensive Read**   **Actual Time** I spent reading: _____

9 **Inquiry Questions**   Questions, ideas, opinions, discoveries:

10 **Synthesis**   Pull it together:

11 **Integrate**   The relationship between the new information and my previous knowledge and experience is:

12 **Assessment**   The following affected (positively or negatively) the quality of my reading performance and how I can improve:

INSTRUCTOR FEEDBACK
Strengths:
Areas for Improvement:
Insights:

Student Success Toolbox

Reading Log

Book/Title, Pages
"The Top Medical Breakthroughs of 2007" *Prevention.* January 2008: 162-169. 7 short pages

Name Paula
Date April 12

1. My purpose is: Reading for my own interest and pleasure & practice using a Read Log

2. My learning objectives are:
To see what medical information is being published through popular sources like Prevention magazine.

To see if there were any breakthroughs I hadn't heard of yet.

I'd also like to practice reading efficiently.

3. My performance criteria are:
Attain basic knowledge of the medical breakthroughs, enough to discuss them superficially, at least.

4. Time I expect to spend reading: 20 minutes

5. Key Vocabulary — Use each key word in a new context or phrase.

I didn't come across any new vocabulary. It's a very popular source and doesn't include any technical or special terms.

6. Outline of reading (structure):

Intro
1. Listing of breakthroughs
   a. Links to additional information
   b. Some symptom listings
2. Listing of upgrades (tools that got better)
3. Hopes and innovations
   a. Links to additional information
4. Final overview with links for each

7. Quick read (information about the reading and questions I have as I begin to read):

This magazine is written primarily for women, and the breakthroughs highlighted focus on women in the "sandwich" generation between children and aging parents.

Questions:
What are considered medical breakthroughs?
How do some people get their medical information?
How much is "prevention" stressed in a magazine with that name?
Is there anything I'd like to look into more deeply?

continued on other side

Improving Learning and Performance through Assessment

8 **Comprehensive Read** **Actual Time** I spent reading: **About 25 minutes**

9 **Inquiry Questions**   Questions, ideas, opinions, discoveries:

I wonder how much this kind of popular article influences people's own health awareness?

How many of these "breakthroughs" will produce profits for the pharmaceutical companies?

10 **Synthesis**   Pull it together:

The article outlines "medical breakthroughs" of 2007, mainly in the areas of cancer, osteoarthritis, and strokes. Many of the "breakthroughs" should now be standard procedure with a thorough medical check up.

11 **Integrate**   The relationship between the new information and my previous knowledge and experience is:

The underlying message seems to be that we should all be advocates for our own health, especially women in the "sandwich" generation, who tend to ignore their own health. This very much echoes the experience I'm accumulating in working with public health even in my currently limited role.

I'd like to do a researched essay on how people get their medical information, and whether or not this makes them more vocal advocates for their own health care.

12 **Assessment**   The following affected (positively or negatively) the quality of my reading performance and how I can improve:

Because of the format of several small sections, I skimmed the piece quickly. I did go back to read a few sections more carefully and followed up on some of the links, but the article was not challenging enough to engage me very deeply.

INSTRUCTOR FEEDBACK

Strengths:	**Reading objectives:** These were clear, compelling, and transferable to other reading situations.
Areas for Improvement:	**Connecting with prior knowledge:** Strive to make your reading summary more concrete and memorable by weaving in some of your prior knowledge of tests, treatments, and conditions.
Insights:	**Tool customization:** The different sections are prompts for critical thinking; some will be more powerful triggers for a reading and it is appropriate to invest more time responding to these.

Name _____

Focus or Course _____

Learning Journal

What I learned:	**What triggered the learning?**
How do I know I've learned it? (validate your learning)	**Why is it important?**
How will I apply my new knowledge *now*?	**How can I apply my learning in the future?**

Copyright © 2013 Pacific Crest

Name _____

Focus or Course _____

Learning Journal

What I learned:	**What triggered the learning?**
How do I know I've learned it? (validate your learning)	**Why is it important?**
How will I apply my new knowledge *now*?	**How can I apply my learning in the future?**

Copyright © 2013 Pacific Crest

Name _____

Focus or Course _____

Learning Journal

What I learned:	**What triggered the learning?**
How do I know I've learned it? (validate your learning)	**Why is it important?**
How will I apply my new knowledge *now*?	**How can I apply my learning in the future?**

Copyright © 2013 Pacific Crest

Name: Don Mapleton
Focus or Course: Math 110

Learning Journal

What I learned:
I learned how to calculate gas mileage in miles driven per gallon of gas (Miles Per Gallon: MPG).

What triggered the learning?
This was part of the current chapter in my math textbook; the context is multiplication and division of whole numbers.

How do I know I've learned it? (validate your learning)
I have worked the practice problems in the math book and arrived at correct answers. In the world outside my math book, I was able to validate the Miles per Gallon for my car. I looked up the MPG for my make and model car (an average of 26 miles per gallon) and I filled the tank and drove 416 miles on that tank of gas. Doing the division, my gas tank should hold 16 gallons. I looked it up in my owner's manual and it does!

Why is it important?
Being able to calculate how many miles I can drive on a given amount of gas will come in very handy, since I live on a budget. I was thinking of trading in my car for another to save money on gas but I see that I already get more miles per gallon than I would in the car I was thinking of buying. I also know that one of the signs that something is wrong with a car is when the gas mileage drops. If I keep a record of my MPG, this will help me keep my car running well. That's important because I depend on my car.

How will I apply my new knowledge *now*?
I will continue to practice working these problems in anticipation of the upcoming math test.

How can I apply my learning in the future?
I will be able to apply this learning when I need to budget for fuel, whether in my normal driving or for something like a road trip. I will be able to calculate how much it will cost me to drive a given number of miles, because if I know how far I drive, through figuring out how many gallons that takes, I can multiply the cost of gas (per gallon) to find out how much it will cost to drive that distance.

Student Success Toolbox

Mentoring Planning

Name _____   Date _____

Need for Mentoring (Areas for Growth)

Establishing

Who have you selected as a mentor?

Why?

What is your relationship to this person?

How will you approach this person about the possibility of a mentoring relationship?

What are your goals? *(What do you want to accomplish with the mentoring relationship?)*

How will you know you're making progress? *(What is your assessment plan?)*

Maintenance

How often will you meet with your mentor?

How will you celebrate growth and improvement?

Closure

How will you celebrate final success?

How will you end the mentoring relationship?

Improving Learning and Performance through Assessment

Mentoring Agreement

We voluntarily enter into a mentoring relationship from which we both expect to benefit. We want this to be a successful relationship, leading to increased growth and performance. We have agreed upon the following terms for our relationship.

Objectives (what we intend to achieve)

_____

_____

_____

_____

_____

_____

_____

_____

Confidentiality

Any sensitive issues that we discuss will be held in confidence. Issues which are off-limits in this relationship include: _____

Frequency of Meetings

We intend to meet at least _____ time(s) each _____. If either party cannot attend a previously scheduled meeting, we agree to notify one another in advance.

Duration

We will continue our mentoring relationship as long as we both feel comfortable and that we are meeting our objectives or until: _____

No-Fault Termination

We are committed to open and honest communication in our relationship. We will discuss and resolve any conflicts as they arise. If, however, either of us needs to terminate the relationship for any reason, we agree to abide by one another's decision.

_____   _____
Mentor   Mentee

_____   _____
Date   Date

Team Tools

Introduction to Forming Teams and Team Roles

Reflector Report

Recorder Report

Weekly Reflector Report

Weekly Recorder Report

Forming Teams

Because cooperative learning and functioning within teams is a key component of many courses, it is important to become familiar with both the consideration of various roles when designing teams as well as the performance criteria of the respective roles.

The typical workplace has become much more team-oriented over the past two decades, underlining the importance of students learning to work well in teams. Students who participate in team environments are much better prepared to succeed both in further education, as well as on the job, than are those without teaming experience. Although it is not yet common for business or industry to employ formal process-oriented roles for team members, graduates who have used roles frequently in undergraduate courses realize that the use of roles would dramatically improve team performance.

Why Roles are Important

- Using roles helps team members to become interdependent and to be individually accountable for team success

- It helps students increase their learning skills, and speed up the four stages of team development: forming (goal setting), storming (conflict resolution), norming (problem-solving), and performing

- Roles should be rotated frequently so that each student has the opportunity to practice each role and to realize that effective learning requires that teams use a variety of roles simultaneously. Rotating roles discourages dominance by one person and gives all students opportunities to practice social, communication, and leadership skills.

Captain

1. Facilitate the team process, keeping it enjoyable and rewarding for all team members.
2. Make sure each member has a role and is performing within that role.
3. Ensure that all team members can articulate and apply what has been learned.
4. Manage time, stress, and conflict.
5. Accept accountability for the overall performance of the team.
6. Contribute to the group as an active learner.

Recorder

1. Record group roles and instructions at the beginning of a task or activity.
2. During an activity, record and collect important information and data, integrating and synthesizing different points of view.
3. Document group decisions and discoveries legibly and accurately.
4. Accept accountability for the overall quality of the Recorder's Report.
5. Control information flow and articulate concepts in alternative forms if necessary.
6. Contribute to the group as an active learner.

Student Success Toolbox

Spokesperson

1. Speak for the team when called upon to do so.
2. Ask questions or request clarification for the team.
3. Make oral presentations to the class for the team.
4. Use the Recorder's journal to share the team's discoveries and insights.
5. Collaborate periodically with the Recorder.
6. Contribute to the group as an active learner.

Technology Specialist

1. Use the available technological tools for the team activity.
2. Listen, converse, and collaborate with team members; synthesize inputs, try suggestions and/or follow directions for the technology.
3. Retrieve information from various sources; manage the available resources and information.
4. Help team members understand the technology and its use.
5. Be willing to experiment, take risks, and try things.
6. Contribute to the group as an active learner.

Planner

1. Review the activity, develop a plan of action, and revise the plan to ensure task completion.
2. Monitor the team's performance against the plan and report deviations.
3. Contribute to the group as an active learner.

Reflector

1. Assess performance, interactions, and the dynamics among team members, recording strengths, improvements, and insights.
2. Be a good listener and observer.
3. Accept accountability for the overall quality of the Reflector's journal.
4. Present an oral Reflector's Report positively and constructively if asked to do so.
5. Intervene with suggestions and strategies for improving the team's processes.
6. Contribute to the group as an active learner.

Optimist

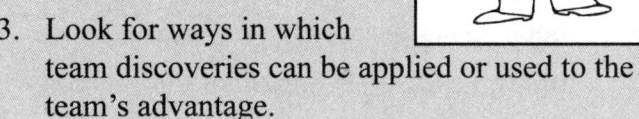

1. Focus on why things will work.
2. Keep the team in a positive frame of mind.
3. Look for ways in which team discoveries can be applied or used to the team's advantage.
4. Contribute to the group as an active learner.

Timekeeper

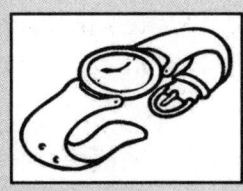

1. Observe the time resource for the activity and/or record the time allocation announced by the facilitator.
2. Keep track of the elapsed time for various tasks and notify the Captain when the agreed-upon time has expired.
3. Contribute to the group as an active learner.

Improving Learning and Performance through Assessment

Critical Thinker

1. Listen critically to group members and ask for clarification and examples, when needed.
2. Make logical connections among people's ideas to increase everyone's learning.
3. Ask timely questions when the quality of thinking can be enhanced.
4. Challenge ideas when they are problematic.
5. Constantly seek ways to increase the quality of thinking by team members.
6. Seek to produce clarity of learning by ensuring effective thinking.
7. Contribute to the group as an active learner.

Conflict Resolver

1. Make sure that team members are respectful to each other.
2. Ensure that each team member is heard and acknowledged, and ensure that issues between people are not ignored.
3. Check that decisions made by the team are consistent with the team's desired outcomes.
4. Contribute to the group as an active learner.

Spy

1. Eavesdrop on other teams during an activity to gather information and seek clarification or direction.
2. Relay information that can help the team perform better.
3. Contribute to the group as an active learner.

A Written Reflector's Report should

- be concise, clear, and accurate
- cite specific examples to convey meaning
- refer to key skills used by the team
- provide supporting documentation
- document affective/emotional issues
- prioritize the most important information
- focus on areas identified in the performance criteria

An Oral Reflector's Report should

- be delivered loudly and clearly enough for all others to hear
- present information concisely (within about 30 seconds, unless specified otherwise)
- identify one strength of the team's performance and explain why it is a strength
- identify one area for improvement that the team can focus on and explain how the improvement can be made
- provide one insight gained about the learning process and explain the significance of the insight

A Written Recorder's Report should

- record accurate information
- identify the team's most important discoveries
- summarize the processes used by the team and identify the context
- identify the concepts and tools used by the team

Student Success Toolbox

Name _____
Team _____
Date _____
Activity _____

Reflector's Report

1 Team Performance

Our team's greatest strength and why: _____
_____
_____
_____

Our team's greatest area for improvement and how the improvement can be made: _____
_____
_____
_____

An insight gained about learning during this activity: _____
_____
_____

2 Individual Performance

Name: _____ Team Role: _____
Strength: _____
Area for Improvement: _____

Name: _____ Team Role: _____
Strength: _____
Area for Improvement: _____

Name: _____ Team Role: _____
Strength: _____
Area for Improvement: _____

Name: _____ Team Role: _____
Strength: _____
Area for Improvement: _____

Instructor Feedback

Strengths:

Areas for Improvement:

Insights:

Copyright © 2013 Pacific Crest

Reflector's Report

Name _____
Team _____
Date _____
Activity _____

1 Team Performance

Our team's greatest strength and why: _____
_____
_____

Our team's greatest area for improvement and how the improvement can be made: _____
_____
_____

An insight gained about learning during this activity: _____
_____

2 Individual Performance

Name: _____ Team Role: _____

Strength: _____

Area for Improvement: _____

Name: _____ Team Role: _____

Strength: _____

Area for Improvement: _____

Name: _____ Team Role: _____

Strength: _____

Area for Improvement: _____

Name: _____ Team Role: _____

Strength: _____

Area for Improvement: _____

Instructor Feedback

Strengths:

Areas for Improvement:

Insights:

Name _____
Team _____
Date _____
Activity _____

Reflector's Report

1 Team Performance

Our team's greatest strength and why: _____
_____
_____
_____

Our team's greatest area for improvement and how the improvement can be made: _____
_____
_____
_____

An insight gained about learning during this activity: _____
_____
_____

2 Individual Performance

Name: _____ Team Role: _____

Strength: _____

Area for Improvement: _____

Name: _____ Team Role: _____

Strength: _____

Area for Improvement: _____

Name: _____ Team Role: _____

Strength: _____

Area for Improvement: _____

Name: _____ Team Role: _____

Strength: _____

Area for Improvement: _____

Instructor Feedback

Strengths:

Areas for Improvement:

Insights:

Copyright © 2013 Pacific Crest

Name: Sandra
Team: Sandra, Ken, Fred, Sam
Date: 4/15
Activity: Team Roles Presentation

Reflector's Report

1. Team Performance

Our team's greatest strength and why: We were able to overcome our obstacles. People on the team were great about stepping in when there was an obvious need.

Our team's greatest area for improvement and how the improvement can be made: Use Perception Checking more frequently — our team realized that our planning was limited to assigning roles, prepared our presentation without feedback, and used limited communication about the presentation. The instructor assessment feedback helped significantly so we will ask for feedback sooner.

An insight gained about learning during this activity: Going down blind alleys but then listening and making changes is how we improve. You have to try something before you can get feedback.

2. Individual Performance

Name: Sam   **Team Role:** Captain
Strength: Is very sensitive to people feeling appreciated and part of the team
Area for Improvement: Slow down when details need to be grasped by everyone.

Name: Jennifer   **Team Role:** Spokesperson
Strength: Knows how to hold an audience's interest with voice and gestures
Area for Improvement: Produce messages for a specific time period (be aware of time).

Name: Ken   **Team Role:** Recorder
Strength: Has a lot of experience he is willing to share to help the team
Area for Improvement: Be more assertive in contributing to the team learning.

Name: Sandra   **Team Role:** Reflector
Strength: Troubleshooting — figuring out what isn't working
Area for Improvement: Intervene on team process at least three times per activity.

Instructor Feedback

Strengths:

Areas for Improvement:

Insights:

Student Success Toolbox

Recorder's Report

Name
Team
Date
Activity

1 Before the activity

Record the basic agenda or plan as outlined by the team leader:

2 During the activity

Important information to be documented:

continued on other side

3 During the activity

Important information to be referenced. Where did you get key information? _____

_____
_____
_____
_____
_____
_____

4 At the end of the activity

State the three most important discoveries learned from the activity along with the significance of each and how each can be applied.

1. _____
_____
_____
_____
_____
_____

2. _____
_____
_____
_____
_____
_____

3. _____
_____
_____
_____
_____
_____

Instructor Feedback

Strengths:

Areas for Improvement:

Insights:

Name
Team
Date
Activity

Recorder's Report

1 Before the activity

Record the basic agenda or plan as outlined by the team leader:

2 During the activity

Important information to be documented:

Copyright © 2013 Pacific Crest

continued on other side

During the activity

Important information to be referenced. Where did you get key information? _____

_____
_____
_____
_____
_____
_____

At the end of the activity

State the three most important discoveries learned from the activity along with the significance of each and how each can be applied.

1. _____
_____
_____
_____
_____
_____

2. _____
_____
_____
_____
_____
_____

3. _____
_____
_____
_____
_____
_____

Instructor Feedback

Strengths:

Areas for Improvement:

Insights:

Name: Charles
Team: Team #4
Date: Jan. 13
Activity: The Terminology of Information Technology

Recorder's Report

1. Before the activity

Record the basic agenda or plan as outlined by the team leader: Our team will be creating a class glossary of information technology terms. There are 4 of us in the team, so we will split the Vocabulary list of 60 words evenly among the 4 of us. Each person will use the suggested resources (dictionary and the internet) to find definitions. We will each use MS Word and create a document so we can merge the lists into a single document. Everyone agreed to send me their lists by e-mail and I will be responsible for creating, saving, and printing the final document which I will bring to class.

2. During the activity

Important information to be documented: Each team member will create a Word document that lists his or her 15 words. Definitions for each term will be added below each term. The source of the definition should be included in parentheses after the definition.

continued on other side

3 During the activity

Important information to be referenced. Where did you get key information? The activity lists a dictionary, and the internet as the resources we should use. As a team we have decided to try locating definitions first in a dictionary, then on the internet. We will only use the internet if we cannot find a definition in the dictionary. We will all note the resource where we found each definition in parentheses after the definition.

4 At the end of the activity

State the three most important discoveries learned from the activity along with the significance of each and how each can be applied.

1. We learned that there is a lot more to most of these terms than we had thought. Every one of us ended up reading more than just definitions we found. So many of the terms do relate directly to other terms.

2. We all also learned that even a dictionary published in the last year was "behind the times" with respect to some of the terms. Technology moves more quickly than the recording of that technology EXCEPT by or in that technology. This means that if you're using software, for example, the best place to find information about the software will be IN the software (the help menu or web-based information on the company web site).

3. We learned that it is a good idea to double-check that everyone understands their individual assignments before the group splits up. Two team members looked up the same list of words! We did not make sure that everyone understood which words they were responsible for. From now on, when we do a similar activity where we split up for everyone to do their own part, each of us will announce his or her assignment out loud, to the whole group.

Instructor Feedback

Strengths:

Areas for Improvement:

Insights:

Student Success Toolbox

Team Members _____
_____
_____
Date _____

Weekly Reflector's Report

Team Productivity

Our three greatest **accomplishments** or strengths this week were:

1. _____

2. _____

3. _____

Our three most important **areas for improvement** along with how we plan to make these improvements are:

1. _____

2. _____

3. _____

Our biggest challenge for completing our work effectively and in a timely manner was: _____

Our plan for overcoming this challenge is: _____

The most important resource we need to complete our work effectively and in a timely manner is: _____

Copyright © 2013 Pacific Crest

continued on other side

2 Improved Team Performance

Compared to last week, our team has made improvements with respect to: _____
_____
_____
_____
_____

3 Team Support of Individual Growth

Which team member(s) grew the most as a learner this week? Explain. _____
_____
_____

Which team member(s) contributed the most to the team's work this week? In what ways? _____
_____

4 Team Dynamics

We had the most fun this week when we: _____
_____
_____

We worked most productively when we: _____
_____
_____

Our biggest conflict was: _____
_____
_____

We resolved the conflict by: _____
_____
_____

The most important teamwork issue we need to address in the future is: _____
_____
_____

Instructor Feedback

Strengths:

Areas for Improvement:

Insights:

Student Success Toolbox

Team Members _____
_____
_____
Date _____

Weekly Recorder's Report

1. Vocabulary

What were the most important vocabulary terms learned by the team this week? Explain the terms in your own words.

_____
_____
_____
_____
_____
_____
_____
_____
_____

2. Resources

Identify the three most valuable resources used by the team this week:

1. _____

2. _____

3. _____

3. Knowledge Table

Build a Knowledge Table of the course for the past week.

Describe key **concepts** learned:

_____
_____
_____
_____
_____
_____

Explain the **processes** developed or improved:

_____
_____
_____
_____
_____
_____

Copyright © 2013 Pacific Crest

continued on other side

Identify **tools** used: _____

_____

_____

_____

_____

_____

_____

Define **contexts** for application: _____

_____

_____

_____

_____

_____

_____

4 Discoveries

Identify your team's three greatest discoveries or understandings gained this week.

1. _____

_____

_____

2. _____

_____

_____

3. _____

_____

_____

5 Remaining Issues

What are your team's two most important questions to be answered or concerns to be addressed?

1. _____

_____

_____

2. _____

_____

_____

What concept, process, tool, or context does your team want to explore in greater detail? _____

_____

_____

Instructor Feedback

Strengths:

Areas for Improvement:

Insights:

Performance Improvement Tools

Continuum of Performance Levels

SII Self-Assessment Report

SII Performance Assessment Report

SII Team Assessment Report

**Getting a Handle on Performance:
The Performance Model**

Performance Analysis and Assessment Preparation Worksheet

Improving Learning and Performance through Assessment

Continuum of Performance Levels

	Knowledge	Social Interactions	Attitude	Abilities
Level 5 *Star Performers*	Can construct and modify models; are valued and respected by experts in the field	Create movements and organizations that often become self-perpetuating	Control their destiny and can control their emotions in challenging situations	Have highly developed learning and research abilities that enable them to excel
Level 4 *Self-Starters*	Are able to add to the knowledge in their discipline	Use relationships effectively to attain success for themselves and others	Seek greater challenges and responsibilities to perform at a higher level and push the boundaries of their own performance	Are able to cultivate new abilities in unfamiliar areas
Level 3 *Responsive Individuals*	Use their problem-solving, learning, and thinking skills to improve their performance and obtain higher-quality results	Are positive people whom others enjoy being around and want to have on their teams	React to challenges with improved performance rather than complaints, feeling good about their accomplishments	Are able to learn from how other people function in a particular area
Level 2 *Content Individuals*	Are satisfied with their modest levels of effort in gaining knowledge	Interact freely with family and friends, but do not seek more diverse contacts and more challenging relationships	Feel like a cog in the machinery, doing little more than what is asked, feeling their contributions are not very significant	Have enough critical thinking and analytic abilities to perform some degree of problem-solving
Level 1 *Static Individuals*	Try to minimize or avoid the effort needed to gain knowledge	Limit their social interactions to like-minded individuals who complain about what they are not getting out of life	Feel that whatever they do will have little impact, that most things are not worth the effort	Must have explicitly defined rules, procedures and policies; need to be prompted to finish something

Student Success Toolbox

Name _____

Focus _____

Time period or activity _____

Self-Assessment

1 The following were my two greatest **strengths** along with the reasons **why** or **how** they were my strengths:

1. _____
   _____

2. _____
   _____

2 My two areas for **improvement**, followed by short and long-term **action plans** explaining **how** I plan to improve are:

1. _____
   _____

   Short-term plan _____
   (now) _____

   Long-term plan _____
   (in future) _____

2. _____
   _____

   Short-term plan _____
   (now) _____

   Long-term plan _____
   (in future) _____

3 An **assessment** of my performance against previous action plans indicates **progress** in the following areas:
_____
_____

My personal **growth** was most enhanced by doing: _____
_____

The reasons **why** I grew are: _____
_____

My mood and **attitude** toward learning during this time was: _____
_____

The most valuable **insight** I learned about myself is: _____
_____

Knowing this will **improve** my performance by: _____
_____

Instructor Feedback

Strengths:

Areas for Improvement:

Insights:

Copyright © 2013 Pacific Crest

49

Name _____
Focus _____
Time period or activity _____

Self-Assessment

1 The following were my two greatest **strengths** along with the reasons **why** or **how** they were my strengths:

1. _____
   _____

2. _____
   _____

2 My two areas for **improvement**, followed by short and long-term **action plans** explaining **how** I plan to improve are:

1. _____
   _____

   Short-term plan _____
   (now) _____

   Long-term plan _____
   (in future) _____

2. _____
   _____

   Short-term plan _____
   (now) _____

   Long-term plan _____
   (in future) _____

3 An **assessment** of my performance against previous action plans indicates **progress** in the following areas:
_____
_____

My personal **growth** was most enhanced by doing: _____
_____

The reasons **why** I grew are: _____
_____

My mood and **attitude** toward learning during this time was: _____
_____

The most valuable **insight** I learned about myself is: _____
_____

Knowing this will **improve** my performance by: _____
_____

Instructor Feedback

Strengths:

Areas for Improvement:

Insights:

50   Copyright © 2013 Pacific Crest

Name _____
Focus _____
Time period or activity _____

Self-Assessment

1 The following were my two greatest **strengths** along with the reasons **why** or **how** they were my strengths:

1. _____
_____

2. _____
_____

2 My two areas for **improvement**, followed by short and long-term **action plans** explaining **how** I plan to improve are:

1. _____
_____

    Short-term plan _____
    (now) _____

    Long-term plan _____
    (in future) _____

2. _____
_____

    Short-term plan _____
    (now) _____

    Long-term plan _____
    (in future) _____

3 An **assessment** of my performance against previous action plans indicates **progress** in the following areas:
_____
_____

My personal **growth** was most enhanced by doing: _____
_____

The reasons **why** I grew are: _____
_____

My mood and **attitude** toward learning during this time was: _____
_____

The most valuable **insight** I learned about myself is: _____
_____

Knowing this will **improve** my performance by: _____
_____

Instructor Feedback

Strengths:

Areas for Improvement:

Insights:

Name: Ashley
Focus: my work
Time period or activity: Writing a draft of an assigned paper

Self-Assessment

1. The following were my two greatest **strengths** along with the reasons **why** or **how** they were my strengths:

1. I was able to use a variety of resources to find information about my assigned topic which is helping me make my paper more interesting than it would be without such a variety of different sources.
2. I was able to create a draft of my paper well before the deadline, leaving me time to revise my introduction

2. My two areas for **improvement**, followed by short and long-term **action plans** explaining **how** I plan to improve are:

1. Transform my set of cited resources into the MLA format required for final submittal. Although we only had to turn in a draft list of sources, I didn't use the MLA format. I wasn't familiar with how to list sources that way.

   Short-term plan (now): I will review the specifications of MLA for all the different types of resources that I have.

   Long-term plan (in future): I will purchase a guide to MLA format so I can continue to expand my understanding of citing different types of resources.

2. Edit for word usage efficiency – tighten up size without losing any meaning. My draft was too long, by a page. The paper is supposed to be 3 to 5 pages and my draft was 6.

   Short-term plan (now): Through feedback by the instructor, I was able to see where there was redundancy in one whole paragraph and I can synthesize two paragraphs.

   Long-term plan (in future): I will be more direct and active with language thus reducing non-efficient passive phrases

3. An **assessment** of my performance against previous action plans indicates **progress** in the following areas:

I am working more efficiently and am better able to search for information online. That helps a LOT by saving me time!

My personal **growth** was most enhanced by doing: By not just taking notes but carefully reading the information I feel like I really understand more and am more comfortable writing in my own voice *because* I understand.

The reasons **why** I grew are: I stopped trying to keep track of what other people said; I took notes but also thought about the cases they were making. I realized that writing a paper isn't just about writing; it's also about learning.

My mood and **attitude** toward learning during this time was: I started out feeling a bit overwhelmed but discovered that by working hard & worrying less, I was going to meet the deadline even while I was learning. That felt great!

The most valuable **insight** I learned about myself is: Once I understand something, I don't have to just repeat what others have said; I can explain it in my own words and in my own way. When I can do that, I KNOW I've learned something!

Knowing this will **improve** my performance by: Giving me the confidence to stop trying to memorize things and try to understand them instead. I may occasionally get something wrong, but I'm learning and thinking for myself.

Instructor Feedback

Strengths:

Areas for Improvement:

Insights:

Student Success Toolbox

Name _____

Performance _____

Date _____

Performance Assessment

1 Performance Criteria

Performance criteria are standards of performance, clearly and explicitly defined, which allow both the performer and assessor to have a mutually understood set of expectations by which performance may be measured and assessed. Performance criteria provide simple-to-understand, realistic, and measurable values of excellence.

1. _____

2. _____

3. _____

2 Notes

In order to complete a high-quality assessment, it is critical that you closely and carefully observe aspects of the performance with special attention to how the performance meets the established performance criteria.

_____

Copyright © 2013 Pacific Crest

continued on other side

Strengths

Identify the ways in which a performance was of high quality and commendable. Each strength statement should address what was valuable in the performance, why this attribute is important, and how to reproduce this aspect of the performance.

1. _____
_____
_____

2. _____
_____
_____

3. _____
_____
_____

Areas for Improvement

Identify the changes that can be made in the future, between this assessment and the next assessment, that are likely to improve performance. Improvements should recognize the issues that caused any problems and mention how changes could be implemented to resolve these difficulties.

1. _____
_____
_____

2. _____
_____
_____

3. _____
_____

Insights

Identify new and significant discoveries/understandings that were gained concerning the performance area; i.e., What did the assessor learn that others might benefit from hearing or knowing? Insights include why a discovery/new understanding is important or significant and how it can be applied to other situations.

_____
_____
_____

Instructor Feedback

Strengths:

Areas for Improvement:

Insights:

Name _____

Performance _____

Date _____

Performance Assessment

1 Performance Criteria

Performance criteria are standards of performance, clearly and explicitly defined, which allow both the performer and assessor to have a mutually understood set of expectations by which performance may be measured and assessed. Performance criteria provide simple-to-understand, realistic, and measurable values of excellence.

1. _____

2. _____

3. _____

2 Notes

In order to complete a high-quality assessment, it is critical that you closely and carefully observe aspects of the performance with special attention to how the performance meets the established performance criteria.

_____

Copyright © 2013 Pacific Crest

continued on other side

Strengths

Identify the ways in which a performance was of high quality and commendable. Each strength statement should address what was valuable in the performance, why this attribute is important, and how to reproduce this aspect of the performance.

1. _____

2. _____

3. _____

Areas for Improvement

Identify the changes that can be made in the future, between this assessment and the next assessment, that are likely to improve performance. Improvements should recognize the issues that caused any problems and mention how changes could be implemented to resolve these difficulties.

1. _____

2. _____

3. _____

Insights

Identify new and significant discoveries/understandings that were gained concerning the performance area; i.e., What did the assessor learn that others might benefit from hearing or knowing? Insights include why a discovery/new understanding is important or significant and how it can be applied to other situations.

_____

Instructor Feedback

Strengths:

Areas for Improvement:

Insights:

Name: Sam Bohn
Performance: Meghan's presentation on her chemistry research
Date: Oct. 15

Performance Assessment

1. Performance Criteria

Performance criteria are standards of performance, clearly and explicitly defined, which allow both the performer and assessor to have a mutually understood set of expectations by which performance may be measured and assessed. Performance criteria provide simple-to-understand, realistic, and measurable values of excellence.

1. Organization of presentation (how appropriate was it with respect to the audience and how complete was it — i.e., was it missing any critical elements?)

2. Quality of data presented (how scientifically sound were the methods used to obtain the data?)

3. Ability to answer questions from the audience (was an answer given and how accurate was that answer?)

2. Notes

In order to complete a high-quality assessment, it is critical that you closely and carefully observe aspects of the performance with special attention to how the performance meets the established performance criteria.

Strong opening with good eye-contact. Slides used appropriately; slide #4 contained chemical formulas probably not explained thoroughly enough for audience, some look confused. Strong use of peer reviewed journal articles but probably pitched a bit beyond an undergraduate audience. Meghan is an interesting speaker & the audience wants to better understand. Lab experiences fully documented and written up nicely. This is high quality work! Question time: Meghan cited Study A when I think she meant Study D. That's a problem. Strong answers but rely too much on technical terminology that is frustrating listeners. Strong answer to question & interesting/provocative answer. Meghan doesn't seem comfortable with audience questions and seems to be a bit flustered. 5 questions asked, 3 very strong answers given, 1 incorrect answer (I think she simply misspoke but it is still incorrect), 1 question not answered. Is losing connection with audience. Gave a good 'next steps' conclusion. Audience gave polite applause; Meghan gracious in response.

continued on other side

Improving Learning and Performance through Assessment

Strengths

Identify the ways in which a performance was of high quality and commendable. Each strength statement should address what was valuable in the performance, why this attribute is important, and how to reproduce this aspect of the performance.

1. Organized: the presentation had all components, sequenced effectively for the audience, with appropriate pacing of content, and associated visuals.

2. Evidenced based: the presentation illustrated the methods used, experimental practices, data collected, and inferences based on sound data analysis with effective graphics

3. Interactivity: the presentation provided opportunity for audience to question and challenge the research, questions rephrased for understanding, and responses that addressed effectively questions or issues to produce greater understanding for all in the audience

Areas for Improvement

Identify the changes that can be made in the future, between this assessment and the next assessment, that are likely to improve performance. Improvements should recognize the issues that caused any problems and mention how changes could be implemented to resolve these difficulties.

1. Match the complexity of the presentation to your audience. The presentation was too complex for this audience. Provide definitions for the more technical terms and present conclusions without using disciplinary language that this non-technical audience didn't understand.

2. Maintain more composure when fielding questions. In listening to questions, take on their perspective, rephrase to gain understanding for what they are asking and then enter a teacher mode where you are helping them to learn and understand better.

3. Also related to the audience questions, consider rephrasing the question (checking perceptions) to make sure that the question that has been asked is the question you're answering. This will help your answers be as responsive as possible.

Insights

Identify new and significant discoveries/understandings that were gained concerning the performance area; i.e., What did the assessor learn that others might benefit from hearing or knowing? Insights include why a discovery/new understanding is important or significant and how it can be applied to other situations.

In assessing Meghan's performance, I was able to identify why I also have some trouble connecting with an audience. I become accustomed to using certain terms and need to be more sensitive to whether my audience has the context for those terms to be meaningful.

Instructor Feedback

Strengths:

Areas for Improvement:

Insights:

Student Success Toolbox

Team Assessment

Name _____

Team Members _____

Date _____

1 The following were our team's two greatest **strengths** along with the reasons **why** or **how** they were our strengths:

1. _____
   _____
   _____

2. _____
   _____
   _____

2 Our two areas for **improvement**, followed by short and long-term **action plans** explaining how we plan to improve are:

1. _____
   _____

   Short-term plan _____
   (now) _____

   Long-term plan _____
   (in future) _____

2. _____
   _____

   Short-term plan _____
   (now) _____

   Long-term plan _____
   (in future) _____

3 Our top three insights into working together as a team are (use the reverse of this form if necessary):

_____
_____
_____
_____
_____
_____

Instructor Feedback

Strengths:

Areas for Improvement:

Insights:

Copyright © 2013 Pacific Crest

Name _____

Team Members _____

Date _____

Team Assessment

1 The following were our team's two greatest **strengths** along with the reasons **why** or **how** they were our strengths:

1. _____
   _____
   _____

2. _____
   _____
   _____

2 Our two areas for **improvement**, followed by short and long-term **action plans** explaining how we plan to improve are:

1. _____
   _____

   Short-term plan _____
   (now) _____

   Long-term plan _____
   (in future) _____

2. _____
   _____

   Short-term plan _____
   (now) _____

   Long-term plan _____
   (in future) _____

3 Our top three insights into working together as a team are (use the reverse of this form if necessary):

_____
_____
_____
_____
_____
_____

Instructor Feedback

Strengths:

Areas for Improvement:

Insights:

Copyright © 2013 Pacific Crest

Team Assessment

Name _____

Team Members _____

Date _____

1 The following were our team's two greatest **strengths** along with the reasons **why** or **how** they were our strengths:

1. _____
_____
_____

2. _____
_____
_____

2 Our two areas for **improvement**, followed by short and long-term **action plans** explaining how we plan to improve are:

1. _____
_____

Short-term plan _____
(now) _____

Long-term plan _____
(in future) _____

2. _____
_____

Short-term plan _____
(now) _____

Long-term plan _____
(in future) _____

3 Our top three insights into working together as a team are (use the reverse of this form if necessary):

_____
_____
_____
_____
_____

Instructor Feedback

Strengths:

Areas for Improvement:

Insights:

Copyright © 2013 Pacific Crest

Name: Robert
Team Members: Robert, Laura, Terri, Julian
Date: March 23

Team Assessment

The following were our team's two greatest **strengths** along with the reasons **why** or **how** they were our strengths:

1. We are able to compensate for one another. When Terri had a death in the family, Julian temporarily took over her tasks. When I had a major paper due, Laura was willing to hold the team meeting and give me notes afterward. Though it is best when we're all present, that isn't always possible. Being able to count on others really makes it easier.

2. Everyone on the team is great about communicating with the other team members. Though I'm the team captain, it is great that Julian set up an online chat room and EVERYONE participates. Everyone gets heard and we all seem to be comfortable sharing our thoughts and ideas. Not having to tip-toe around or worry about 'the quiet one' is nice.

Our two areas for **improvement**, followed by short and long-term **action plans** explaining how we plan to improve are:

1. Strengthen performance within roles. Casual use of roles, especially not using the forms very effectively has limited growth of team performance

   Short-term plan (now): Will pair team roles so the pair member will assess the other's filled out form. Captain-Reflector and Recorder-Spokesperson.

   Long-term plan (in future): Focus self-assessment on performing within a role. Use the performing in a team rubric to assess & analyze each performance to strengthen a very specific dimension of role performance during each activity.

2. Come to effective team consensus. During last activity, our team was split between two completely different responses and had to submit two different responses.

   Short-term plan (now): Differentiate if responses are based upon values or opinions which justifies multiple responses, otherwise determine the critical inquiry question to clarify the issue separating the responses.

   Long-term plan (in future): Long-term: Use compare and contrast learning skills better to see how the positions are similar and what is really different (once identified, have the Skeptic challenge premises and logic development)

Our top three insights into working together as a team are (use the reverse of this form if necessary):

I think we've all found that despite our moments of stress as a team, that working together means being able to do more than you can on your own. Having someone who is able to lend a hand when you're not able to do it all on your own is amazing and makes us all grateful that we have gotten to know each other. This is a VERY positive team experience which we ALL appreciate.

Instructor Feedback

Strengths:

Areas for Improvement:

Insights:

Student Success Toolbox

Getting a Handle on Performance: The Performance Model

The Theory of Performance allows us to dissect a performance. Through this lens, we see that a performance is comprised of the following dimensions: identity, skills, knowledge, context, personal factors, and fixed factors. A performer has some control over all of these, with the exception of fixed factors.

```
  IDENTITY
  SKILLS
  KNOWLEDGE
  CONTEXT
  PERSONAL FACTORS
+ FIXED FACTORS
─────────────────
= PERFORMANCE
```

Identity	As individuals mature in a discipline, they take on the shared identity of the professional community while elevating their own uniqueness. For a learner to perform well, he or she must have a strong identity as a member of a learning community. A student demonstrates identity as a learner when engaging in learning activities, such as attending classes and studying. A student who is majoring in psychology begins to demonstrate identity within that field by using the terminology of psychology.
Skills	Skills describe specific actions that are used by individuals, groups, or organizations in multiple types of performances. Within education, the focus is on those skills that are transferable across contexts and allow individuals to improve their mastery of subject matter. These are known as *learning skills*. Learners who perform well work to increase their mastery of learning skills.
Knowledge	Knowledge involves facts, information, concepts, theories, or principles acquired by a person or group through experience or education. You are learning about the Performance Model right now and are adding to your knowledge with every word you read.
Context	This component includes variables associated with the situation in which the individual or organization performs. Each time you perform as a learner, you do so within a specific context, which includes a number of variables. For example, your performance in this course has as its context the way you meet (in a classroom? online?), how often you meet as a class, the length of the term (a full semester? an intensive summer course?), and so on.
Personal Factors	This component includes variables associated with the personal situation of an individual. Your performance as a student depends a great deal upon your personal factors and your life situation. To use a simple example, how well are you able to study if you're tired because you worked late last night? Personal factors can present a significant challenge to performing well.
Fixed Factors	This component includes variables unique to an individual that cannot be altered. This is the only aspect of performance that cannot be altered and includes items such as the first language you learned, color-blindness, etc. While your performance as a learner is certainly affected by fixed factors. Assuming that your performance is constrained by these factors is a mistake.

Improving Learning and Performance through Assessment

Performance Analysis and Assessment
(based on the Performance Model)

Name _____ **Date** _____

Performance _____

Identity
Describe the Identity: _____
_____

How will awareness of **identity** help to improve the performance? _____
_____
_____

Learning Skills
Describe the key Learning Skills: _____
_____

How will improving these **skills** help to improve the performance? _____
_____
_____

Knowledge
Describe the Knowledge: _____
_____

How will increasing the level of **knowledge** help to improve the performance? _____
_____
_____

Context
Describe the Context: _____
_____

How will awareness of **context** help to improve the performance? _____
_____
_____

Personal Factors
Describe the existing Personal Factors: _____
_____

How might the **personal factors** be addressed in order to help improve the performance? _____
_____
_____

Fixed Factors
Describe the Fixed Factors: _____
_____

Can awareness of **fixed factors** help to improve the performance? How? _____
_____
_____

Performance Analysis and Assessment
(based on the Performance Model)

Name _____ **Date** _____

Performance _____

Identity
Describe the Identity: _____
_____

*How will awareness of **identity** help to improve the performance?* _____
_____
_____

Learning Skills
Describe the key Learning Skills: _____
_____

*How will improving these **skills** help to improve the performance?* _____
_____
_____

Knowledge
Describe the Knowledge: _____
_____

*How will increasing the level of **knowledge** help to improve the performance?* _____
_____
_____

Context
Describe the Context: _____
_____

*How will awareness of **context** help to improve the performance?* _____
_____
_____

Personal Factors
Describe the existing Personal Factors: _____
_____

*How might the **personal factors** be addressed in order to help improve the performance?* _____
_____
_____

Fixed Factors
Describe the Fixed Factors: _____
_____

*Can awareness of **fixed factors** help to improve the performance? How?* _____
_____
_____

Improving Learning and Performance through Assessment

Performance Analysis and Assessment
(based on the Performance Model)

Name Breanna Apple **Date** October 16

Performance Writing a first literary work for publication: The Sorcerer's Stone

Identity — Describe the Identity: J.K. Rowling, though comfortable with the act of writing didn't identify herself as a writer; she trained to be a teacher.

How will awareness of **identity** help to improve the performance? In identifying as an author or writer, one generally has access to the support of other writers.

Learning Skills — Describe the key Learning Skills: imagining, making connections, producing humor

How will improving these **skills** help to improve the performance? The writing integrates complexity with simplicity of creating (by imagining) new context and images that tie together. She consistently produces humor to contrast tension.

Knowledge — Describe the Knowledge: Rowling did a lot of research about wizards and magic, even using Latin in naming fictional plants and spells.

How will increasing the level of **knowledge** help to improve the performance? According to Rowling, her mother died while she was writing the book. She felt such loss and sadness and put that in the book as Harry's loss. Increased knowledge allows authors to make believable characters.

Context — Describe the Context: Most of Rowling's writing was done in cafes in Edinburgh. She wrote her manuscript using an old manual typewriter.

How will awareness of **context** help to improve the performance? Knowing her context, she was able to plan how to use the time and resources she had available most efficiently. Rather than waiting until she could afford a computer, she used what she had and got the work done.

Personal Factors — Describe the existing Personal Factors: Rowling was a newly single mother, with a baby, who was surviving on welfare & going to school nearly full-time.

How might the **personal factors** be addressed in order to help improve the performance? Her personal factors contributed to the book taking longer to finish. Perhaps there were some alternatives? Daycare? A helpful relative? She did a good job balancing everything & just kept writing.

Fixed Factors — Describe the Fixed Factors: No known fixed factors.

Can awareness of **fixed factors** help to improve the performance? How? If you know your fixed factors, then you can take them into account and find ways to work around them. If her hands were paralyzed, for instance, she could have dictated the story and paid an assistant to type it.

Preparation Worksheet

Implementing the Preparation Methodology

Name _____

Step	Explanation
1 Clarify performance *(describe)*	
Identity	Who are you as a performer (e.g., dancer, orator, teacher, etc.)?
Learning Skills	Which learning skills are critical to the performance?
Knowledge	What knowledge must you have to perform successfully?
Context	What is the context of the performance?
Personal Factors	What personal variables must you deal with to perform successfully?
Fixed Factors	What variables must you compensate for?
2 Define outcomes	
3 Define expectations *(yours and the audience's)*	

Copyright © 2013 Pacific Crest

continued on other side

67

Step	Explanation
4 Identify stressors *(describe issues or reasons)*	
5 Review and assess readiness *(describe how)*	
6 Rehearse *(describe how)*	
7 Create view of success *(describe)*	
8 Commit to performing *(describe how)*	
9 Perception check *(how did you know you were—or were not—on target to meet performance outcomes?)*	
10 Self-assess	

COMPLETE AFTER PERFORMANCE (sidebar for steps 9–10)

Student Success Toolbox

Preparation Worksheet

Implementing the Preparation Methodology

Name Charles Nakagawa

Step	Explanation
1 Clarify performance *(describe)*	I will give a 12 to 15 minute speech to the incoming freshman class, during orientation week. The topic of my speech will be the challenges I experienced in my first year of college.
Identity	Who are you as a performer (e.g., dancer, orator, teacher, etc.)? I am a student with a full year of college behind me.
Learning Skills	Which learning skills are critical to the performance? preparing, rehearsing, organizing a message, sharing knowledge
Knowledge	What knowledge must you have to perform successfully? I need to know my audience and their expectations and remember experiences from my first year of college.
Context	What is the context of the performance? Sharing personal experiences with fellow students
Personal Factors	What personal variables must you deal with to perform successfully? I'm nervous about speaking in public.
Fixed Factors	What variables must you compensate for? I'm not very tall and the podium is good-sized. I will need to make sure there's a step or block for me to stand on so that I can see everyone & they can see me.

2 Define outcomes

I will take 12 to 15 minutes and deliver an interesting speech that gives my audience some potentially useful information to think about that might be able to help them as they face the challenges of their first year of college.

3 Define expectations *(yours and the audience's)*

My expectations are that I will get through this, not make any major mistakes, come across as someone just like them, and maybe through sharing my experiences, help someone else. Their expectations are probably to be minimally entertained in the time between their orientation to student services and lunch. If they are like I was, they'll be more interested to hear from students than from professors when it comes to what college is like for students.

Improving Learning and Performance through Assessment

Step	Explanation
4 Identify stressors *(describe issues or reasons)* 12 to 15 minutes seems like a lot of time to fill with speaking in public. I'm stressed about coming up with enough to talk about. I'm also stressed about standing up in front of several hundred people and speaking.	
5 Review and assess readiness *(describe how)* I will know that I'm ready for this when I can recall the outline of my speech and deliver each section with only one or two sort glances at my note cards.	
6 Rehearse *(describe how)* I will draft an outline of my speech and give it to my sister and a couple of her high school friends. I also plan to practice my speech in front of a camera and then to play it back and self-critique my presentation.	
7 Create view of success *(describe)* The audience will applaud my efforts and my orientation contact will thank me for my input. Further proof of my success could be one or more of the students who listen to the speech coming up to me afterward, say next semester, and speaking with me about some of what I shared.	
8 Commit to performing *(describe how)* I've agreed to give the speech and have approved the electronic copy of the program that gives an overview of who I am and when I'll be speaking. I have also written about 3/4 of my outline.	

COMPLETE AFTER PERFORMANCE

9 Perception check *(how did you know you were—or were not—on target to meet performance outcomes?)* While I was speaking, I noticed a lot of eye-contact and when I shared more humorous experiences, I heard a lot of good-natured laughter. It was obviously going well!	
10 Self-assess WOW. I'm so relieved it is over but really glad I agreed to do it. I gave a strong performance and was an interesting speaker. The information I shared seems to have touched people; I've had several people thank me for sharing and ask for more information. Surprisingly, I almost ran out of time; I hadn't considered that there might be questions from the audience. The next time I give a speech like this, I'll be sure to find out if there is an expectation of audience participation (Q&A). I was also pretty nervous, though I just went ahead with the speech. I think I could use more experience speaking in front of people and should probably ask if I can take a turn as group spokesperson in my biology group. Overall, it seems to have been a good and valuable experience, for everyone.	

Course Tools

How to be an "A" Student

Course Record Sheet

Weekly Planner

Blank Calendar

Beginning: Learning Contract

Analyzing a Course Syllabus (Activity)

Mid-Term: Mid-Term Assessment

Closure: Course Assessment

Classification of Learning Skills

How to be an "A" Student

1. **Clarify shared expectations in the course**
   Ask, "What is expected of me?" and "What do I expect of myself?" (Tool: *Analyzing a Course Syllabus Activity*)

2. **Create a plan of action**
   Determine how you will meet the course expectations. (Tool: *Analyzing a Course Syllabus Activity*)

3. **Make your commitment to success in writing**
   Share it with another person. (Tool: *Learning Contract*)

4. **Prepare for class by reading for learning**
   Don't just read; read and think and ask questions. (Tool: *Reading Log* or notes with inquiry questions)

5. **Think critically in class**
   Ask or write down inquiry questions, connecting what you are learning to what you already know. Follow up on any questions that remain once class is over. Find the answers to your questions.

6. **Teach someone else**
   Pass along your learning to someone else as a way to test your understanding.

7. **Demonstrate your learning and increased understanding before the next class meeting**
   Use it or lose it. Find ways to use what you have learned.

8. **Extend your knowledge**
   Create a new problem to solve or try applying your learning in a new context.

9. **Anticipate future challenges so there are no surprises**

10. **Execute readiness preparation for every performance task**
    For a test, take a practice test; for an essay, write a draft. Find a way to practice or rehearse.

11. **Let go of your fear and stress**
    Finish your preparation for a performance such as a test not less than 24 hours before the performance. Studies have proven that relaxing and getting plenty of rest before performing yields better results than cramming or practicing up until the last minute.

12. **Engage in assessment and self-assessment after every performance**
    Regular assessment of your performance by both yourself and others will help you strengthen and improve your performance. (Tools: *Assessment Forms*)

Course Record Sheet

Course Name	Tests	Quizzes	Homework & Assignments

Improving Learning and Performance through Assessment

Course Record Sheet

Course Name	Tests	Quizzes	Homework & Assignments

Weekly Planner for the Week of: _____

	Sun	Mon	Tues	Wed	Thurs	Fri	Sat
7:00 am							
8:00 am							
9:00 am							
10:00 am							
11:00 am							
12:00 pm							
1:00 pm							
2:00 pm							
3:00 pm							
4:00 pm							
5:00 pm							
6:00 pm							
7pm-7am							

Improving Learning and Performance through Assessment

Weekly Planner for the Week of: _____

	Sun	Mon	Tues	Wed	Thurs	Fri	Sat
7:00 am							
8:00 am							
9:00 am							
10:00 am							
11:00 am							
12:00 pm							
1:00 pm							
2:00 pm							
3:00 pm							
4:00 pm							
5:00 pm							
6:00 pm							
7pm-7am							

Month: _____

Sun	Mon	Tues	Wed	Thurs	Fri	Sat

Improving Learning and Performance through Assessment

Month: _____

Sun	Mon	Tues	Wed	Thurs	Fri	Sat

Month: _____

Sun	Mon	Tues	Wed	Thurs	Fri	Sat

Improving Learning and Performance through Assessment

Activity: Analyzing a Course Syllabus

Learning skills: *clarifying expectations, inquiring, prioritizing*

Why

A well-written syllabus provides you with important information about a course including learning objectives, benefits to the student, content to be covered, important dates, and the basis for determining your grade. The syllabus involves an understood agreement between you and the instructor about what you will be expected to learn, the processes utilized to help you learn, and how you will be evaluated. By reading and analyzing the syllabus for a course, you know what to expect and where to concentrate your efforts to gain the most from that course.

Learning Objectives

1. Get a complete picture of this course including what your instructor expects from you.
2. Determine what you want from this course and how you are going to get it.

Performance Criteria

Criterion #1: the inquiry questions produced concerning the syllabus

Attributes:
a. formulation of at least three questions
b. the answers to the formulated questions cannot be found in the syllabus
c. answers to the questions are relevant to this course and have significant value to other students

Criterion #2: a plan of action for the course

Attributes:
a. includes clear obtainable goals to achieve from the course
b. includes tasks and associated hourly efforts required to meet goals
c. lists the top five priorities for success

Plan

1. Obtain a copy of the syllabus for this course.
2. Answer the Critical Thinking Questions.
3. Write three inquiry questions that you would like answered about this course.
4. After your instructor decides how to address these questions (either through an in-class or online discussion or a consulting session), record the answers to the questions.
5. Write a plan of action for how you will be a successful student in this course.

Critical Thinking Questions

1. What are the main sections of the syllabus?

2. List all the resources that you will use in this course.

3. What are the prerequisites (background knowledge, required skills, qualities, or attitudes) for this course?

4. Of the main topics covered in this course, which ones are of most interest to you? Why?

5. How will your grade be determined in this course?

6. What are the four most important things you believe a successful student must do to learn the most and to earn the best possible grade in this course?

   -
   -
   -
   -

Improving Learning and Performance through Assessment

Inquiry questions about the syllabus

Plan of action for the course

Learning Contract

As a student in this course, I commit to:

1. Take risks
2. Work hard alone and with others
3. Take responsibility for my performance
4. Wanting and working to improve my performance
5. Fully participate in class
6. Prepare for every class
7. Be proactive, not passive
8. Be open to new situations
9. Be willing to assess performance
10. Not judge others' values
11. _____
12. _____
13. _____
14. _____
15. _____

Printed Name: _____

Signed: _____

Date: _____

Feel free to use this page for notes!

Mid-term Assessment

Name _____ Date _____

1. What are the three greatest strengths of the course? Why do you consider these strengths?

   -
   -
   -

2. What are three of the most important things you have learned related to your team and personal goals?

   -
   -
   -

3. What are three improvements that could be made to help you and others learn and perform better in the process of meeting your goals?

   -
   -
   -

4. What are three important topics that still need to be covered during this course?

   -
   -
   -

Copyright © 2013 Pacific Crest

continued on other side

5. What have you learned about cooperative learning and teamwork, and how have you contributed to help others learn and grow?

6. What action plans can you and your team put in place that will help you meet your stated goals?

7. What have you learned about your own learning process?

8. Assess the effectiveness of this course in producing desired course outcomes.

Additional comments or questions you would like answered:

Course Assessment

Name _____ Date _____

1. Review the Course Outcomes or Goals as presented in your course syllabus. Note each outcome/goal below and assess to what degree that outcome/goal was met.

   Outcome/Goal   **Degree to which it was met**

   _____   _____
   _____   _____
   _____   _____
   _____   _____
   _____   _____
   _____   _____

2. What are the three greatest strengths of the course? Why do you consider these strengths?

   •

   •

   •

3. What are three aspects of the course that you feel could be improved to help students meet course outcomes/goals?

   •

   •

   •

4. How do you plan to use what you have learned in this course?

   •

   •

   •

space for additional feedback is available on the reverse of this page

Improving Learning and Performance through Assessment

Additional feedback:

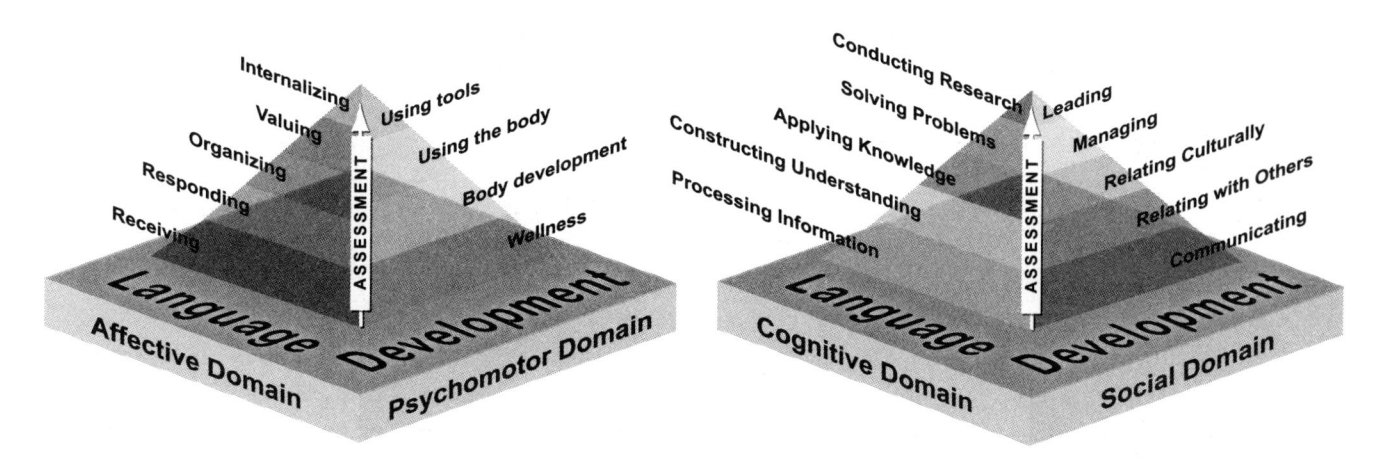

The Classification of Learning Skills
for Educational Enrichment and Assessment

Affective Domain: Receiving, Responding, Organizing, Valuing, Internalizing
Psychomotor Domain: Wellness, Body development, Using the body, Using tools
Cognitive Domain: Processing Information, Constructing Understanding, Applying Knowledge, Solving Problems, Conducting Research
Social Domain: Communicating, Relating with Others, Relating Culturally, Managing, Leading

(Each pyramid shows Language Development and Assessment as unifying dimensions.)

The Classification of Learning Skills for Educational Enrichment and Assessment (CLS) represents a 15-year research effort by a team of process educators who created this resource to assist with the holistic development of their students. Used by both faculty and students, the CLS is a valuable tool which helps to identify key processes and skills fundamental to learning. It also provides the framework for making quality assessments of performance and serves as a guide for improving assessment and self-assessment skills.

Faculty who teach using active learning formats will find this resource especially useful when measuring, assessing, and improving student performance. Students can use the CLS to identify the most important skills required to perform at the level of a skilled practitioner in various content areas.

What is a Learning Skill?

Learning skills are discrete entities that are embedded in everyday behavior and operate in conjunction with specialized knowledge. They can be consciously improved and refined. Once they are, the rate and effectiveness of overall learning increases. They can be identified at an early stage of a learner's development. No matter what the person's age or experience, learning skills can be improved to higher levels of performance through self-assessment, self-discipline, or guidance by a mentor. This growth in learning skill development is usually triggered by a learning challenge of some kind and is facilitated by actions built on a shared language between mentor and mentee.

Development of the Classification

Initial work on The Classification of Learning Skills focused on the cognitive domain, looking primarily at critical thinking and problem solving skills. Benjamin Bloom's Taxonomy of Educational Objectives served as a resource during the construction of the cognitive domain. Efforts to build the social domain coincided with research projects such as the SCANS Report (*Secretary's Commission on Achieving Necessary Skills*), which pointed out the need to help students develop communication, teamwork, and management skills. Daniel Goleman's seminal work on emotional intelligence profoundly informed the work on the affective domain learning skills. The CLS was further expanded when levels for learner performance were identified and terms such as "enhanced learner" and "self-grower" were introduced.

Cognitive Domain

Processing Information

Collecting Data *(from a disorganized source)*
 Observing, Listening, Skimming, Memorizing, Recording, Measuring

Generating Data *(to fill a void)*
 Predicting, Estimating, Experimenting, Brainstorming

Organizing Data *(for future use)*
 Filtering, Outlining, Categorizing, Systematizing

Retrieving Data *(from an organized source)*
 Recognizing patterns, Searching, Recalling, Inventorying

Validating Information *(for value)*
 Testing perceptions, Validating sources, Controlling errors, Identifying inconsistency, Ensuring sufficiency

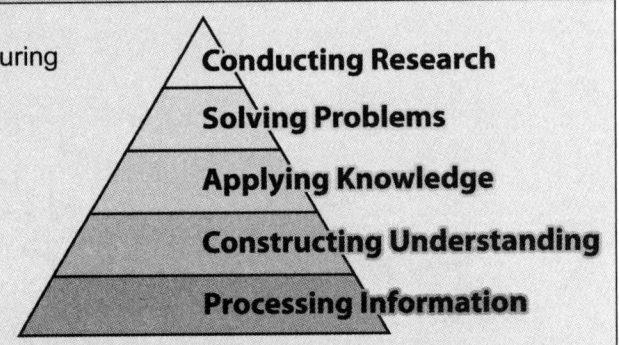

Pyramid (top to bottom): Conducting Research, Solving Problems, Applying Knowledge, Constructing Understanding, Processing Information

Constructing Understanding

Analyzing *(characterizing individual parts)*
 Identifying similarities, Identifying differences, Identifying assumptions, Inquiring, Exploring context

Synthesizing *(creating from parts)*
 Joining, Integrating, Summarizing, Contextualizing

Reasoning *(revealing meaning)*
 Interpreting, Inferring, Deducing, Inducing, Abstracting

Validating Understanding *(for reliability)*
 Ensuring compatibility, Thinking skeptically, Validating completeness, Bounding

Applying Knowledge

Performing with Knowledge *(in real context)*
 Clarifying expectations, Strategizing, Using prior knowledge, Transferring

Modeling *(in abstract context)*
 Analogizing, Exemplifying, Simplifying, Generalizing, Quantifying, Diagramming

Being Creative *(in new contexts)*
 Challenging assumptions, Envisioning, Linear thinking, Divergent thinking, Transforming images, Lateral thinking

Validating Results *(for appropriateness)*
 Complying, Benchmarking, Validating

Solving Problems

Identifying the Problem *(to establish focus)*
 Recognizing the problem, Defining the problem, Identifying stakeholders, Identifying issues, Identifying constraints

Structuring the Problem *(to direct action)*
 Categorizing issues, Establishing requirements, Subdividing, Selecting tools

Creating Solutions *(for quality results)*
 Reusing solutions, Implementing, Choosing alternatives, Harmonizing solutions

Improving Solutions *(for greater impact)*
 Generalizing solutions, Ensuring robustness, Analyzing risks, Ensuring value

Conducting Research

Formulating Research Questions *(to guide inquiry)*
 Locating relevant literature, Identifying missing knowledge, Stating research questions, Estimating research significance, Writing measurable outcomes

Obtaining Evidence *(to support research)*
 Designing experiments, Selecting methods, Extracting results, Replicating results

Discovering *(to expand knowledge)*
 Testing hypotheses, Reasoning with theory, Constructing theory, Creating tools

Validating Scholarship *(for meaningful contribution)*
 Defending scholarship, Responding to review, Confirming prior work, Judging scholarship

Student Success Toolbox

Social Domain

Communicating

Receiving a Message
Attending, Reading body language, Responding, Checking perceptions

Preparing a Message
Defining purpose, Knowing the audience, Organizing a message, Selecting word usage, Formatting a message, Illustrating

Delivering a Message
Selecting a venue, Generating presence, Sharing knowledge, Persuading, Storytelling, Managing transitions

Relating with Others

Inviting Interaction
Taking an interest in others, Initiating interaction, Hosting, Expressing positive nonverbal signals, Assisting others, Being non-judgmental

Relating for Meaning
Belonging, Befriending, Empathizing, Collaborating, Parenting, Mentoring

Performing in a Team
Goal setting, Achieving consensus, Planning, Cooperating, Compromising

Performing in an Organization
Accepting responsibility, Being assertive, Making proposals, Documenting, Influencing decisions

Relating Culturally

Accepting Constraints
Obeying laws, Inhibiting impulses, Noticing social cues, Recognizing conventions

Living in Society
Sharing traditions, Supporting institutions, Valuing communities, Reacting to history, Being a citizen

Demonstrating Cultural Competence
Clarifying stereotypes, Appreciating cultural differences, Generalizing appropriately, Using culture-specific expertise

Managing

Managing People
Building consensus, Motivating, Modeling performance, Assessing performance, Evaluating performance

Building and Maintaining Teams
Defining team roles, Setting rules, Delegating authority, Confronting poor performance, Recruiting, Mediating

Managing Communication
Connecting with stakeholders, Networking, Marketing, Sustaining change

Managing Resources
Negotiating, Politicking, Securing resources, Creating productive environments

Leading

Envisioning
Projecting the future, Seeing implications, Balancing perspectives, Responding to change

Building a Following
Inspiring, Sharing a vision, Generating commitment, Maintaining integrity

Maintaining Commitment
Meeting individual needs, Taking meaningful stands, Thinking opportunistically, Being charismatic

Empowering
Giving credit, Encouraging ownership, Grooming subordinates, Being a servant leader

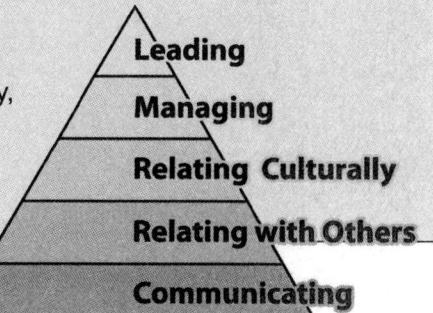

Improving Learning and Performance through Assessment

Affective Domain

Receiving (Being Open to Experience)

Exploring Self
  Observing self, Listening to self, Perceiving reactions, Body awareness, Identifying emotions

Exploring Surroundings
  Being curious, Being open, Being positive, Being playful, Being active

Experiencing Emotions
  Feeling loved, Grieving, Feeling joyful, Laughing, Responding to aesthetics, Feeling secure

Responding (Engaging in Life)

Emoting
  Loving, Caring, Respecting, Giving, Comforting

Addressing Life's Changes
  Coping, Persisting, Accepting help, Believing in oneself, Responding to failure, Appreciating evaluation

Leveraging Life's Successes
  Responding to success, Being humble, Seeking assessment, Celebrating, Acknowledging others

Organizing (Managing Oneself)

Regulating Self
  Responding to requests, Recognizing dissonance, Managing dissonance, Managing resources, Prioritizing, Being self-disciplined

Managing Performance
  Being decisive, Committing to the future, Preparing, Rehearsing, Challenging standards, Being self-efficacious, Orchestrating emotions

Managing Emotions
  Modulating emotions, Recognizing emotional contexts, Preparing for future emotions, Modeling emotions

Valuing/Cultivating Values

Valuing Self
  Building identity, Evolving a personal philosophy, Trusting self, Caring for self, Reflecting

Valuing Natural Laws
  Appreciating diversity, Valuing nature, Valuing family/significant others, Being spiritual

Refining Personal Values
  Identifying values, Exploring beliefs, Clarifying one's value system, Validating values, Aligning with social values, Accepting ownership

Internalizing

Synergizing Feelings
  Associating feelings, Interpreting feelings, Analyzing feelings, Predicting feelings, Objectifying emotions, Exploring emotions

Facilitating Personal Development
  Recognizing personal potential, Seeking assessment, Seeking mentoring, Being patient

Challenging Self
  Exploring potential, Expanding identity, Being courageous, Being proactive, Growing culturally, Being empathic

Committing Beyond Self
  Committing to caring, Accepting outcomes, Acting on beliefs, Enhancing self-esteem, Maturing, Self-actualizing

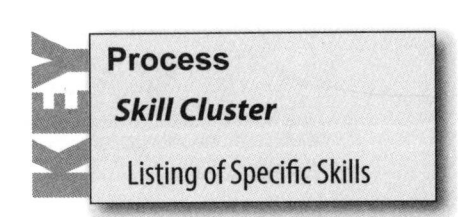

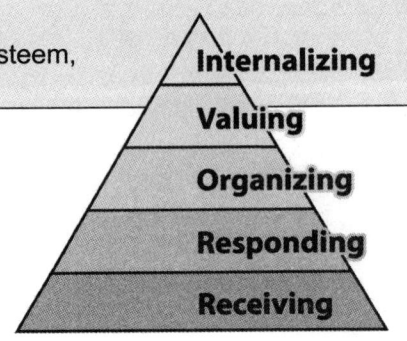

KEY

Process

Skill Cluster

Listing of Specific Skills

Pyramid (bottom to top): Receiving, Responding, Organizing, Valuing, Internalizing